Let's Chat!

ESL Dialogues

Beginner

by
Barbara Agor
Stewart Agor
Martha Hansen

Frank Schaffer Publications®

Authors: Barbara Agor, Stewart Agor, Martha Hansen
Development House: Words & Numbers
Design and Production: Ophelia M. Chambliss

Frank Schaffer Publications®

Send all inquiries to:
Frank Schaffer Publications
8720 Orion Place
Columbus, Ohio 43240

Let's Chat!: ESL Dialogues—Beginner

ISBN: 0-7682-3076-4

3 4 5 6 7 8 9 10 PAT 13 12 11 10 09

Contents

To the Helper

How might a helper use these dialogues with English language learners?

This book contains dialogues at beginning speaking and reading levels for students of a variety of ages (grades 3–8). Some of these dialogues may be more appropriate for older students than younger. Please read each dialogue before using, and choose those that are most appropriate for the students in your class. Here are some tips for using these dialogues with beginning students.

1. Allow simple listening. The principal section of each dialogue sequence (marked with an audio CD icon) is recorded on the companion audio CD.

2. Connect listening with understanding. Just listening to meaningless dialogues is not very helpful. Start with some short dialogues that can be paired with a series of actions, such as "Make a Face" or "Making Play Dough." Learners can listen and understand.

3. Encourage memorization, but only a little. Grabbing a bit of language, repeating it, and feeling the way it sounds and rolls over the tongue gets language inside the mind and the body. However, there is no need for learners to memorize everything, and forcing them to do so could be counterproductive. Instead, encourage them to pick out the words and phrases that come easily, that have particular meaning for them, or that just sound good. Also help them identify those words, phrases, and sentences that are more difficult but seem likely to be useful to them as they negotiate their daily lives in a new language. Then let the rest of the dialogue wash over them. They will absorb much more than they realize.

4. Combine reading and speaking. A strategy called "read and look up" provides wonderful support for students who are able to read in English. They select a dialogue or part of a dialogue to recite. They may look at the page as much and as often as they want. However, when they speak, they must look up, and not look at the book. At first, students may only be able to speak a few words at a time before they need to consult the book again in order to lurch forward with a few more words. Soon they will begin to put words and phrases together in meaningful chunks, and, before they know it, they will manage whole lines.

5. Encourage students to build variations. Some of the dialogues are followed by variations. These variations provide additional practice but also serve as guides to students about how they might further adapt a dialogue.

6. Focus on the story. With their predictable structure of beginning, middle, and end, stories provide a scaffold for understanding. Many of the dialogues in this book can be read as stories, in which the opening dialogue and its continuations pose a problem and work toward a solution. Give learners the opportunity to agree or disagree with the solution in the dialogue. That will lead them to discuss, rethink, rewrite, re-enact, or transform the dialogue in ways that are meaningful to them.

7. Promote transformations of the dialogues. You can also support learners by encouraging them to transform the dialogues into some other form. For students who understand but are not yet comfortable speaking, select some segment of a dialogue and suggest that they pantomime it. For student artists, look for parts of dialogues that they can illustrate. Later, these students or others can rearrange the illustrations, try new sequences, or use the illustrations as prompts to perform parts of the original dialogues.

8. Use the index of language functions. At the end of this book, you will find a listing of language functions that reflect standards established by the international organization TESOL (Teachers of English to Speakers of Other Languages). For easy reference, these functions are indexed to the specific dialogues in which they appear.

Special thanks to Louis Carrillo, Luz M. Aranda, and Ophelia M. Chambliss.

Barbara Agor, Stewart Agor, Martha Hansen

To the Learner

This is your book. We hope that you enjoy it. Here are some tips that we think will help you learn and enjoy learning.

1. You don't have to start at the beginning of the book. Find the dialogues that interest you. Start with ones that are short if you prefer. Or start with long dialogues if they are about something in your life—like solving a problem at home or in school. (The dialogues that are recorded on the audio CD are marked with an audio CD icon in the margin.)

2. When you read or listen to a dialogue, you don't have to understand and remember every single line. Think about it—when you hear people talking, you don't understand every single thing that they say, do you? But some things stick, and you remember them—what they mean and how they sound. These dialogues are no different from real life in this way.

3. When you are reading or listening to a dialogue, you can pay more attention to some parts and less attention to others. How? Use a highlighter to mark a few words or phrases that you would like to be able to say easily and naturally. (If you don't own this book, write the words or phrases on a separate piece of paper.)

4. Find people who will read and practice the dialogues with you. Look at the end of each dialogue, where there are questions, thoughts, and ideas for you and others to talk about. You will think of other ways to practice and expand the dialogue. Do them.

5. Finally, don't give up! We hope this book will add to your good days and will be a helpful friend on your journey toward learning English.

Barbara Agor, Stewart Agor, Martha Hansen

HOME  1

1 A New Puppy

Jasmin, Salim, and Mrs. Rose
In the kitchen

Jasmin: Mom, Sally just got a new puppy.

Mrs. Rose: That's nice.

Jasmin: Puppies are really cute.

Mrs. Rose: Yes, they are.

Jasmin: Umm… Mom… Can I have a puppy?

Mrs. Rose: What do you think?

Jasmin: I think no.

Mrs. Rose: That's right.

Jasmin: But why, Mom?

Mrs. Rose: Who do you think will feed it?

Jasmin: I will, I promise!

Mrs. Rose: Every day?

Jasmin: Yes, every day.

Mrs. Rose: And who will walk with it outside?

Jasmin: Oh, I will. I'll walk with it and run with it.

Mrs. Rose: Every day?

Jasmin: Every day.

Mrs. Rose: Even when it's snowing?

Jasmin: Even when it's snowing.

Mrs. Rose: Even when it's raining?

Jasmin: Even when it's raining.

Mrs. Rose: Even when you're sick?

Jasmin: Well…

Salim: I can help! Not every day, but when Jasmin is sick.

Mrs. Rose: Are you sure?

Salim: Yes, I'm sure. I'd really like a puppy, too.

Mrs. Rose: Well, I'll think about it.

0-7682-3076-4   *Let's Chat: ESL Dialogues*

1a (continuation)

Jasmin, Salim, Mrs. Rose, and Mr. Rose

At the dinner table

Mrs. Rose:	Dear, Jasmin and Salim want a puppy.
Mr. Rose:	Sure, and I want a jet plane.
Jasmin:	No, Dad, I'm serious.
Salim:	We'll take care of it.
Jasmin:	We'll feed it.
Salim:	We'll walk it.
Jasmin:	We'll teach it tricks.
Salim:	It will wait for us after school.
Jasmin:	Yes, Mom and Dad. You two are at work when we come home from school.
Salim:	With a puppy, we won't be lonely!
Mr. Rose:	I don't know…
Mrs. Rose:	Remember when you were a boy in Bosnia?
Mr. Rose:	Oh, yes. Our dog Sasha.
Mrs. Rose:	You said that Sasha was like a brother.
Mr. Rose:	Yes…I loved that dog. *(long pause)* Let me think about it.

1b (continuation)

The next morning

Mrs. Rose:	Wake up, kids!
Jasmin:	Oh, Mom, it's Saturday. I'm sleepy.
Mrs. Rose:	I think you'll want to get up.
Jasmin:	Ten more minutes, please…
Mrs. Rose:	Breakfast is ready.
Jasmin:	I'll eat it cold. Just ten more minutes.
Salim:	Yeah, ten more minutes.
Mr. Rose:	Well, Dear, how long should we wait?
Mrs. Rose:	I don't know. I'm ready to go.
Salim:	Go where?
Mr. Rose:	To the Humane Society.
Jasmin:	What's there?
Mrs. Rose:	Free dogs and puppies…if you see one that you like.
Salim and Jasmin:	We're up!

EXPANSION

Do you have a pet? If you do, make a list of what you do to take care of it and read the list to your teacher. Talk with friends about pets.

2 Lost and Found

Alexander and Mr. Soto

In the living room

Alexander:	Dad, I can't find my CD player.
Mr. Soto:	Where did you use it last?
Alexander:	In the living room. Can you help me look there?
Mr. Soto:	Sure. Did you look behind the sofa?
Alexander:	Yes, but it wasn't there.
Mr. Soto:	Did you look under the table?
Alexander:	Yes, but it wasn't there, either.
Mr. Soto:	Did you look on the bookshelf?
Alexander:	No, not yet. *(pause)* Hey! There it is! Thanks, Dad.

2a (variation)

Pablo and Stephen

In the classroom

Pablo:	Hey, Stephen, have you seen my green pen?
Stephen:	No, I haven't. When did you lose it?
Pablo:	At the beginning of class.
Stephen:	Did you look under your desk?
Pablo:	Yes, but it wasn't there.
Stephen:	Did you look inside your book bag?
Pablo:	Yes, but it wasn't there, either.
Stephen:	Did you look in your notebook?
Pablo:	No, but I'll check now. *(pause)* Hey! There it is! Thanks!
Stephen:	No problem!

EXPANSION

Name something that you have lost and then found. Where did you look for it? Where did you finally find it?

3 It's Mine!

George and Katina (brother and sister)

In the living room

George: Hey, what are you doing with that?

Katina: With what?

George: With that.

Katina: Oh, you mean this?

George: Yeah, that's my shirt.

Katina: Oh, yes, I know it is.

George: So, why are you wearing it?

Katina: My shirts are in the wash.

George: But that's a boy's shirt.

Katina: No problem. Girls can wear boys' shirts.

George: Mom, Katina's wearing my shirt!

3a (variation)
In the driveway

George: Hey, what are you doing with that?

Katina: With what?

George: With that.

Katina: Oh, you mean this?

George: Yeah, that's my bike.

Katina: Oh, yes, I know it is.

George: So, why are you taking it?

Katina: My bike has a flat tire.

George: But that's a boy's bike.

Katina: No problem. Girls can ride boys' bikes.

George: Mom, Katina's taking my bike!

EXPANSION

Tell your teacher about a time when a brother, sister, or friend borrowed something of yours without asking permission.

4 I'm Sleepy, Mom!

Nicole and Mrs. Katsas
At home

Mrs. Katsas:	Nicole, time to get up!
	(silence)
Mrs. Katsas:	Nicole, time to get up!
Nicole:	*(sounding very tired)* What?
Mrs. Katsas:	I said, it's time to get up!
Nicole:	*(still sounding tired)* Do I have to?
Mrs. Katsas:	Yes.
Nicole:	But I'm sleepy, Mom.
Mrs. Katsas:	The bus will be here any minute!
Nicole:	The bus?
Mrs. Katsas:	Oh, no! There it goes!
Nicole:	I'm sorry, Mom.
Mrs. Katsas:	You'll have to stay home. Your dad took the car to work.
Nicole:	But I can't stay home today.
Mrs. Katsas:	Why not?
Nicole:	Because I have to go on a field trip with my class.
Mrs. Katsas:	*(pause)* Maybe my friend Anna can take you.
Nicole:	Thanks, Mom.

4a (continuation)

Mrs. Katsas and Anna
On the telephone

Mrs. Katsas:	Hello? Anna? This is Elena.
Anna:	Hi, Elena. How are you?
Mrs. Katsas:	I'm OK, but I need a favor.
Anna:	What can I do?
Mrs. Katsas:	Can you please give Nicole a ride to school? She overslept and missed the bus.
Anna:	OK. Can she be ready in 20 minutes?
Mrs. Katsas:	Yes, and thank you very much.

EXPANSION

Have you ever missed your bus? Talk to your teacher or to other students about missing buses.

5 Too Loose, Too Tight, or Just Wrong

Alejandro and Mrs. Diaz
In the kitchen

Mrs. Diaz:	Hurry up, Alejandro, you'll be late for school!
Alejandro:	I'm coming!
Mrs. Diaz:	Wait! Breakfast!
Alejandro:	No time, Mom.
Mrs. Diaz:	Hey, wait a minute!
Alejandro:	No time, Mom.
Mrs. Diaz:	Yes, there's time, Alejandro.
Alejandro:	What?
Mrs. Diaz:	Those pants!
Alejandro:	What pants?
Mrs. Diaz:	Those pants.
Alejandro:	What about them?
Mrs. Diaz:	You're not wearing those to school.
Alejandro:	No?
Mrs. Diaz:	No, you're not.
Alejandro:	Oh, Mom, everyone's wearing them.
Mrs. Diaz:	Well, not *my* son. They're too big.
Alejandro:	But I'll be late for school!
Mrs. Diaz:	I don't care. Change those pants.
Alejandro:	But all my new pants are big.
Mrs. Diaz:	Then wear some old ones.
Alejandro:	Do I have to?
Mrs. Diaz:	Yes. And put on a belt.

5a (variation)
Darlene and Mrs. Diaz
In the kitchen

Mrs. Diaz:	Hurry up, Darlene, you'll be late for school!
Darlene:	I'm coming!
Mrs. Diaz:	Wait! Breakfast!
Darlene:	No time, Mom.
Mrs. Diaz:	Hey, wait a minute!
Darlene:	No time, Mom.

Mrs. Diaz: Yes, there's time, Darlene.

Darlene: What?

Mrs. Diaz: Those shorts!

Darlene: What shorts?

Mrs. Diaz: Those shorts.

Darlene: What about them?

Mrs. Diaz: You're not wearing those to school.

Darlene: No?

Mrs. Diaz: You're not.

Darlene: Oh, Mom, everyone's wearing them.

Mrs. Diaz: Well, not *my* daughter. They're too tight.

Darlene: But I'll be late for school!

Mrs. Diaz: I don't care. Change those shorts.

Darlene: Oh…Mom…

5b (variation)

Mrs. Diaz: Hurry up, Darlene, you'll be late for school!

Darlene: I'm coming!

Mrs. Diaz: Wait! Breakfast!

Darlene: No time, Mom.

Mrs. Diaz: Hey, wait a minute!

Darlene: No time, Mom.

Mrs. Diaz: Yes, there's time, Darlene.

Darlene: What?

Mrs. Diaz: What's on your face?

Darlene: My face?

Mrs. Diaz: Your face.

Darlene: Well… Nothing.

Mrs. Diaz: You're not wearing lipstick to school.

Darlene: No?

Mrs. Diaz: You're not.

Darlene: Oh, Mom, everyone's wearing lipstick.

Mrs. Diaz: Well, not *my* daughter. You look awful!

Darlene: But I'll be late for school!

Mrs. Diaz: I don't care. Wash your face.

Darlene: Oh… Mom….

Mrs. Diaz: And we'll talk more when you get home.

Darlene: Do we have to?

Mrs. Diaz: Yes. A serious talk.

EXPANSION

Do you and your parents ever disagree about what you do or wear? What do they say? What do you say? Write your own dialogue with you talking to your parents.

6 Doing Homework

Al and Marty

At Al's house, after school

Al: Hmm… This is kind of interesting.

Marty: What?

Al: My project for school.

Marty: An interesting school project?

Al: Yes, really.

Marty: What is it?

Al: We have to write down everything we watch on TV. For a whole week.

Marty: Well, that would be easy for me.

Al: Why?

Marty: I wouldn't have to write anything. We don't have a TV.

Al: Ha! That's why you're always coming to my house after school.

Marty: Not really. I like coming to your house.

6a (variation)

Al: Hmm… This is kind of interesting.

Marty: What?

Al: My project for school.

Marty: An interesting school project?

Al: Yes, really.

Marty: What is it?

Al: We have to read a picture book to a little kid.

Marty: Well, that would be easy for me.

Al: Why?

Marty: I have five little brothers and sisters. And lots of picture books.

Al: Say, can I come to your house to do my project?

Marty: Sure, my brothers and sisters would love it.

EXPANSION

Describe a school project that you did at home. Explain what you did. Tell your teacher or another student.

7 Family Responsibilities

Cynthia, Roger, and Mrs. Harris

In the living room

Cynthia: Hey, it's Saturday!

Roger: Finally!

Cynthia: Let's watch cartoons!

Roger: Yes, let's. *(sound of cartoon noises on TV)*

Cynthia: Hey, look at that!

Roger: That's funny!

Cynthia: Oh, look at that!

Roger: Watch out!

Cynthia: Uh-oh... *(a cartoon thump or splat)*

Mrs. Harris: Kids, what are you doing?

Roger: Watching cartoons, Mom.

Mrs. Harris: Did you forget something?

Cynthia: Hmmm...

Roger: I don't think so...

Mrs. Harris: It starts with B.

Cynthia: Breakfast?

Roger: No, we had breakfast. Pancakes, remember?

Cynthia: Oh, yeah.

Roger: Brush our teeth?

Cynthia: No, we did that.

Mrs. Harris: Here's a hint: bed.

Cynthia: Oh, I guess we forgot to make our beds.

Roger: Right away, Mom.

7a (variation)

Cynthia: Hey, it's Saturday!

Roger: Finally!

Cynthia: Let's watch cartoons!

Roger: Yes, let's. *(sound of cartoon noises on TV)*

Cynthia: Hey, look at that!

Roger: That's funny!

Cynthia: Oh, look at that!

Roger: Watch out!

Cynthia: Uh-oh... *(a cartoon thump or splat)*

Mrs. Harris:	Kids, what are you doing?
Roger:	Watching cartoons, Mom.
Mrs. Harris:	Did you forget something?
Cynthia:	Hmmm…
Roger:	I don't think so…
Mrs. Harris:	It starts with T.
Cynthia:	Teeth? Brush our teeth?
Roger:	No, we did that after breakfast, remember?
Cynthia:	Oh, yeah.
Roger:	T…T…
Cynthia:	I can't think of anything.
Mrs. Harris:	Here's a hint: trash.
Cynthia:	Oh, I guess we forgot to take out the trash.
Roger:	Right away, Mom.

7b (variation)

Cynthia:	Hey, it's Saturday!
Roger:	Finally!
Cynthia:	Let's watch cartoons!
Roger:	Yes, let's. *(sound of cartoon noises on TV)*
Cynthia:	Hey, look at that!
Roger:	That's funny!
Cynthia:	Oh, look at that!
Roger:	Watch out!
Cynthia:	Uh-oh… *(a cartoon thump or splat)*
Mrs. Harris:	Kids, what are you doing?
Roger:	Watching cartoons, Mom.
Mrs. Harris:	Did you forget something?
Cynthia:	Hmmm…
Roger:	I don't think so…
Mrs. Harris:	It starts with G.
Cynthia:	G…G…
Roger:	Something that starts with G. Something good?
Mrs. Harris:	I think so.
Roger:	G…Then it can't be garbage.
Cynthia:	I can't think of anything.
Mrs. Harris:	Here's a hint: Grandma.
Cynthia:	Oh, that's right! I guess we forgot to call Grandma.
Roger:	Can we do it later? After cartoons?

EXPANSION

Tell your teacher or another student what your chores are at home. Does your mother or father need to remind you to do them? What do they say? What do you say?

8 Making Play Dough

Brian and Jane (his baby-sitter)
In the kitchen of Brian's home

Brian: Jane, look what I got in school!

Jane: What is it?

Brian: It's a recipe. Look!

Jane: Flour, water, salt, oil. Hmmm…

Brian: I think it's easy to make!

Jane: But flour, water, salt, oil. I don't think it would taste very good.

Brian: Oh, I forgot to explain. It's not to eat.

Jane: But if you cook it…

Brian: It's to play with.

Jane: You play with food?

Brian: It's called play dough.

Jane: Play dough…

Brian: You can make things with it. Like little people. Or cats. Can we make it now?

Jane: Let's see. *(slowly)* Flour, water, cream of tartar. And oil, salt, and food coloring. I think your mom has everything.

Brian: Great! Let's go!

8a (continuation)

Jane: OK. First, let's put everything we need on the table.

Brian: OK.

Jane: And we'll need measuring cups and spoons.

Brian: Here they are.

Jane: Good. Now we're ready to go. Read me the recipe.

Brian: Measure 1 cup flour.

Jane: OK.

Brian: Put it in the pan.

Jane: OK.

Brian: Add 1 cup warm water.

Jane: Got it.

Brian: And 2 teaspoons cream of tartar.

Jane: OK.

Brian: 1 teaspoon oil.

Jane: Yep.

Brian: One-quarter cup salt.

Jane: It's in.

Brian: Ugh! What a mess!

Jane: It'll change. What do we do next?

8b (continuation)

Brian: Next we turn on the heat—medium, it says. And stir, and stir, and stir.

Jane: How long do we stir?

Brian: I don't know… Hey, look! It's starting to get smooth.

Jane: It's not very pretty, though.

Brian: Oh, I forgot! Add some food coloring.

Jane: What color do you want?

Brian: Let me think…. Blue or green… Green!

Jane: OK, here it goes. Now stir some more.

Brian: That's better.

Jane: Does the recipe say anything else?

Brian: Remove from heat.

Jane: And I'm remembering to turn off the stove.

Brian: OK. It still doesn't look right, though.

Jane: Let's look at the recipe again. It says to knead it and punch it.

Brian: I can do that.

Jane: Good. Keep kneading.

Brian: OK, but my hands are getting tired.

Jane: Here, I'll do it for a while. *(pause)* Looks done to me.

Brian: Great! Now, let's play. I think I'll make a dinosaur first.

EXPANSION

Write how to do something, step by step. Explain it to someone. See if the person understands and can do it right.

9 Eight Lives to Go

Carmen and Ludmilla (neighbors)
On the street near their houses

Carmen: What's wrong?

Ludmilla: My cat ran away.

Carmen: Are you sure?

Ludmilla: Yes, he's been gone for three days.

Carmen: Did you look around the neighborhood?

Ludmilla: Yes. We even put up signs that said "Lost Cat."

Carmen: Is that all they said?

Ludmilla: No, silly. They told what the cat looked like and gave our address and telephone number.

Carmen: Where did you put the signs?

Ludmilla: *(sounding really sad)* All over.

Carmen: Just look for him. I think he'll come home.

Ludmilla: I hope so.

Carmen: And anyway, they say that cats have nine lives.

9a (continuation)

Carmen: Hi, Ludmilla. Any news about your cat?

Ludmilla: Yes! I heard him last night, meowing outside my window.

Carmen: So what did you do?

Ludmilla: I went outside.

Carmen: Then what?

Ludmilla: I called his name.

Carmen: Then what?

Ludmilla: I called again, and all of a sudden, he appeared!

Carmen: What did you do then?

Ludmilla: I brought him home. He looked starved. He was so hungry that he ate two bowls of food!

Carmen: See? I told you cats have nine lives. But now, he probably has only eight left!

EXPANSION

Ask your classmates if they have ever lost a pet. Ask them to tell you what happened. If you ever lost a pet, tell your classmates about it.

10 A Big Event

Angela and Natasha

On the telephone

Angela:	Guess what!
Natasha:	What?
Angela:	My sister's having a baby!
Natasha:	How exciting! When?
Angela:	I think in May.
Natasha:	Let me see… It's January now…
Angela:	Yes, we have to wait for February…
Natasha:	and March…
Angela:	and April…
Natasha:	and then the baby!
Angela:	I can't wait!

10a (variation)

Natasha:	Guess what!
Angela:	What?
Natasha:	We're buying a house!
Angela:	How exciting! When?
Natasha:	Well, we're buying it now.
Angela:	Wow!
Natasha:	But we can't move in until summer.
Angela:	Let me see… It's March now…
Natasha:	Yes, we have to wait for April…
Angela:	and May…
Natasha:	and June…
Angela:	and then you move!
Natasha:	I can't wait! I'm going to have my own bedroom.

EXPANSION

What are you or your family waiting for? When will it happen? What is good about it?

11 All My Friends Are Going

Dora and Mrs. Patel

In the kitchen

Dora:	Mom, do you know what a sleep-over is?
Mrs. Patel:	A sleep…over…?
Dora:	Yeah, where you sleep at someone else's house.
Mrs. Patel:	Why would anyone do that?
Dora:	Well, it's like a party.
Mrs. Patel:	A party? All night long?
Dora:	Yeah.
Mrs. Patel:	It sounds funny to me.
Dora:	Lucy is having one.
Mrs. Patel:	One what?
Dora:	*(exasperated)* A sleep-over.
Mrs. Patel:	And who is this Lucy?
Dora:	You know Lucy. She's my best friend in school.
Mrs. Patel:	Oh yes, she came for dinner last month.
Dora:	So, can I go to Lucy's sleep-over?
Mrs. Patel:	I don't think so.
Dora:	Why not?
Mrs. Patel:	I don't know. It just sounds funny.
Dora:	Well, it doesn't sound funny to me.
Mrs. Patel:	How would I explain it to your grandmother?
Dora:	That's easy. Don't tell her.
Mrs. Patel:	I don't know. I still don't like the idea.
Dora:	Please, Mom. All my friends are going.
Mrs. Patel:	And if all your friends were going to jump off a bridge, would you jump, too?
Dora:	Mom, you know a sleep-over isn't like that.
Mrs. Patel:	Well, I'll think about it.

11a (continuation)

Dora, Mrs. Patel, and Mr. Patel

At the dinner table

Mrs. Patel: Dear, Dora wants to go on a sleep-over.

Mr. Patel: A sleep-over? What's that?

Mrs. Patel: It's something that they do here.

Dora: Yes. All the girls go to someone's house and sleep there.

Mrs. Patel: It's like a party.

Mr. Patel: A party at night? You sleep there? All night?

Dora: I don't think we sleep much. We laugh and tell stories.

Mr. Patel: Hmmm… Sounds funny to me.

Dora: *(mocking her father's voice)* Sounds funny to me. *(in a normal voice)* Everything here sounds funny to you.

Mrs. Patel: Dora, be careful.

Dora: I'm sorry, Dad. I didn't mean it.

Mr. Patel: Hmph.

Dora: Well?

Mr. Patel: Your Mother and I will talk about it.

Mrs. Patel: But don't get your hopes up.

11b (continuation)

At the breakfast table the next day

Dora: Mom and Dad, did you think about the sleep-over?

Mr. Patel: Yes, Dear, we did.

Dora: And?

Mrs. Patel: I'm sorry, Dear, we just don't feel good about it.

Dora: Awww… Everyone else will be there.

Mrs. Patel: Yes, I know. I'm sorry.

Mr. Patel: But we have an idea.

Dora: An idea? What?

Mr. Patel: After your birthday, what about a sleep-over here?

Dora: Here? At our house?

Mr. Patel: Yes.

Dora: Oh, that would be great! Will you make Grandma's special cake? Everyone will love it!

Mrs. Patel: Of course. And I hope you understand.

Dora: Well, I do… a little.

EXPANSION

Can you think of any activities that are common in North America but that parents from other countries don't understand? Try to list some and share your list with your teacher and classmates.

12 Make a Face

Michael and Yuri
At Michael's house

Michael:	Have you ever made a Halloween pumpkin, Yuri?
Yuri:	Never, Michael. How do you do it?
Michael:	I'll show you. We do it every year.
Yuri:	What do we need?
Michael:	We need a pumpkin, a knife, a marker, a big spoon, some newspaper, and a candle.
Yuri:	Have you got all those things?
Michael:	We sure do! Come on into the kitchen.

12a (continuation)

Yuri:	What should I do first?
Michael:	First draw the face. Use the marker.
Yuri:	OK… There's one eye… And there's the other eye.
Michael:	Good! Now draw a nose.
Yuri:	Nose… Like this?
Michael:	Yup. And finally, draw a mouth. Leave some teeth sticking down from the top and up from the bottom.
Yuri:	OK… there! How does it look?
Michael:	It looks scary! Just right for Halloween.

12b (continuation)

Yuri:	What should I do next?
Michael:	Next you cut the top out. Cut a big square around the stem. Then lift the top off.
Yuri:	Let's see. Like this?
Michael:	Yeah. That's good. Now take the spoon and scoop out all the seeds.
Yuri:	OK. Yuck! They're gross! What should I do with them?
Michael:	Wrap them in the newspaper and throw them away.
Yuri:	Now what do I do?
Michael:	Now you cut out the face where you drew it. Cut holes for the eyes and nose.
Yuri:	Like this?
Michael:	Yes. When you do the mouth, cut carefully around the teeth so they don't break off.
Yuri:	OK... Almost done... There! Hey that looks cool!

12c (continuation)

Michael:	OK. We drew the face, scooped out the seeds and threw them away, cut out the top, and cut the face.
Yuri:	Are we done now?
Michael:	Not quite. There's one more thing we have to do.
Yuri:	What's that?
Michael:	We have to place the candle inside the pumpkin.
Yuri:	OK. There, it's inside.
Michael:	Now light it.
Yuri:	Oh, that looks great!
Michael:	It will be even better tonight when it's dark!

EXPANSION

In North America, people carve faces in pumpkins for Halloween, in late October. Tell your friends what you know about Halloween, and ask them to tell you what they know.

13 The Argument

 *Mikey, Rosa*

At the dinner table

Rosa: Mom, Mikey spilled spaghetti sauce on the carpet!

Mikey: No I didn't! She's always trying to get me in trouble.

Rosa: Yes he did! I saw him do it.

Mikey: I did not!

Rosa: You did too!

Mikey: Did not!

Rosa: Did too!

Mikey: *(getting louder and faster)* Did not!

Rosa: Did too!

Mikey: Did not!

Rosa: Did too!

Mikey: Did not!

(long pause)

Rosa: Michael, don't argue with me. With my very own eyes, I clearly saw that you did *not* spill spaghetti on the carpet.

Mikey: I DID TOO!

Rosa: See, Mom? I told you so.

13a (variation)
In Mr. Adams's class at school

Rosa: Mr. Adams! Mikey didn't do his homework last night!

Mikey: I did too! She's always trying to get me in trouble!

Rosa: No he didn't!

Mikey: I did too!

Rosa: Did not!

Mikey: Did too!

Rosa: Did not!

Mikey: *(getting louder and faster)* Did too!

Rosa: Did not!

Mikey: Did too!

Rosa: Did not!

Mikey: Did too!

(long pause)

Rosa: Mr. Adams, I saw with my own eyes. He sat in front of the television and did his homework, all night long!

Mikey: I DID NOT!

Rosa: See, Mr. Adams? I told you so.

EXPANSION

Rosa wins the argument because she tricks Mikey. How does she do that? Talk about it with your teacher and your friends.

SCHOOL

1 Where Do We Sit?

Jeannie (younger sister), Sarah (older sister), and Mr. Claude

Getting onto the school bus

Sarah & Jeannie:	*(speaking together)* Good morning, Mr. Claude.
Mr. Claude:	Good morning, girls.
Sarah:	*(whispering to Jeannie)* Where do we sit?
Jeannie:	Oh, oh… Not there.
Sarah:	Not where?
Jeannie:	Not over there, next to Brian.
Sarah:	Why not?
Jeannie:	He's mean.
Sarah:	Well, OK. Where, then?
Jeannie:	Oh, oh… Not there!
Sarah:	Not where?
Jeannie:	Not over there, next to David.
Sarah:	Why not?
Jeannie:	He's cute.
Sarah:	OK, I'm confused. Why not sit next to a cute boy?
Jeannie:	He'll think I like him.
Sarah:	I think we'd better just stand up.

1a (variation)

Sarah & Jeannie:	*(speaking together)* Good morning, Mr. Claude.
Mr. Claude:	Good morning, girls.
Sarah:	*(whispering to Jeannie)* Where do we sit?
Jeannie:	Oh, oh… Not there.
Sarah:	Not where?
Jeannie:	Not over there, next to Alice.

21

Sarah: Why not?

Jeannie: She'll take my lunch.

Sarah: Well, OK. Where, then?

Jeannie: Oh, oh... Not there!

Sarah: Not where?

Jeannie: Not over there, next to Bob.

Sarah: Why not?

Jeannie: He likes me.

Sarah: OK, I'm confused. Why not sit next to him?

Jeannie: He'll think *I* like *him*.

Sarah: I think we'd better just stand up.

1b (continuation)

Mr. Claude: Jeannie, Sarah, sit down, please.

Sarah: Come on, Jeannie. Sit down!

Jeannie: But where?

Sarah: Just sit anywhere!

Mr. Claude: Girls...

Sarah: Come on. We're going to be in trouble.

Jeannie: Well, OK, but you first.

Sarah: Not over here...

Jeannie: Stop it! Just sit down!

Mr. Claude: *(in a stern voice)* Girls...

Sarah
& Jeannie: *(together)* We're sitting, Mr. Claude. We're sitting!

1c (continuation)

Jeannie, Sarah, and Bob

Jeannie: Bob, can we sit here?

Bob: Sure, come on.

Jeannie: Thanks.

Sarah: Jeannie, move over. I'm falling out of the seat.

Jeannie: I can't!

Sarah: You can, too.

Jeannie: *(whispering)* No, I can't. Bob's too close!

Sarah: Next time, let's walk to school.

EXPANSION

Where do you sit on the bus? Who sits with you? Make up a dialogue with your friend about where to sit.

2 Can I See?

Al and Bonnie

In the school hallway

Al: What are you looking at, Bonnie?

Bonnie: Oh hi, Al. I'm looking at the pictures from the field trip.

Al: Neat! Can I see?

Bonnie: Here, take a look.

Al: Who's that on the left?

Bonnie: That's Danielle.

Al: Oh, yeah, I see. And who's that next to her?

Bonnie: Hmmm... I can't tell.

Al: It looks like Mary.

Bonnie: No, Mary has longer hair.

Al: Maybe it's Joan.

Bonnie: Yep. It's Joan. I'll show you some more after class.

2a (continuation)
After class

Bonnie: Look at this picture. Remember when we hiked up that hill?

Al: My legs won't let me forget.

Bonnie: Everyone looks so tired!

Al: Hey, look! I'm in that one.

Bonnie: Cute picture.

Al: Do you think you could get me a copy?

Bonnie: Sure. I'll bring one tomorrow.

Al: Thanks Bonnie.

2b (continuation)
Next day, in the hallway

Bonnie: Hi Al. I've brought you the picture.

Al: Great! Can I see it?

Bonnie: Actually, it's in my locker. Are you free now?
We could go get it.

Al: Yes. Where is your locker?

Bonnie: It's on the second floor, near the art room.

Al: Let's go!

EXPANSION

Bring in photos of yourself in some activity like a trip, a party, a wedding, or a vacation. Tell other students what you were doing when the pictures were taken.

0-7682-3076-4   *Let's Chat: ESL Dialogues*

3 Where Are We?

CD - 17

Margaret, Mark, and Mr. Ruby
In Mr. Ruby's classroom

Mr. Ruby:	OK, let's get started. Open your books to the chapter on Manifest Destiny.
	(sound of books opening and pages shuffling)
Margaret:	*(quietly)* Psst…, Mark. What did he say?
Mark	*(also quietly)* Manifest Destiny.
Margaret:	*(in a normal voice)* Manifest what?
Mark:	*(also in a normal voice)* Mr. Ruby means our homework reading.
Mr. Ruby:	Margaret and Mark, do you have a problem?
Mark:	No, Mr. Ruby. Sorry.
Mark:	*(quietly again)* Margaret, it's page 37.
Margaret:	*(quietly)* Got it. Thanks.

3a (continuation)

Margaret and Mark
In the hallway

Margaret:	Hey, Mark, wait a minute.
Mark:	Sure.
Margaret:	Mark, thanks a lot.
Mark:	For what?
Margaret:	For telling me what page.
Mark:	Sure, no problem.

3b (continuation)

Margaret and Janet
On the school bus

EXPANSION

Talk with your teacher about things you can do when you don't understand something in a class.

Margaret:	I felt bad today. Mr. Ruby yelled at us.
Janet:	Mr. Ruby? He's nice. He doesn't yell.
Margaret:	Well, Mark and I were talking. I guess we were too loud. But I didn't understand what Mr. Ruby was saying. So I asked Mark.
Janet:	Too bad. Next time ask Mr. Ruby. He'll help you.
Margaret:	I guess… Say, Janet, what does Manifest Destiny mean, anyway?

4 Oops, I Forgot!

Elizabeth and Juana

Near their lockers, after school

Elizabeth: Hi, Juana. What are you doing tonight?

Juana: Not much.

Elizabeth: Do you want to go to the movies?

Juana: Yeah, but I don't have any money.

Elizabeth: I have a little extra. I could lend you some. When do you think you could pay me back?

Juana: Next week when I get my allowance.

Elizabeth: OK. I'll ask my dad to pick you up at 6:30. Can you be ready then?

Juana: I sure can!

4a (continuation)

Elizabeth and Susan

Two weeks later

Elizabeth: You know, Susan, I hate to say anything bad and you know Juana is my good friend…

Susan: Yes…

Elizabeth: Well, I gave her money for the movies, but she never paid me back.

Susan: So, just ask her! She probably forgot.

Elizabeth: OK. I will. Thanks.

4b (continuation)

Elizabeth and Juana

The next day

EXPANSION

Why did Elizabeth talk to Susan before she asked Juana for the money? Tell your teacher what you think.

Elizabeth: Hi, Juana.

Juana: Oh…hi, Elizabeth. How are you doing?

Elizabeth: OK. I was wondering whether you had the movie money yet?

Juana: Oops! I'm so sorry. I forgot. But I have it here, and I'll give it to you right now.

Elizabeth: Thanks.

Juana: You're welcome. I'm really sorry, Elizabeth.

Elizabeth: It's OK. Don't worry about it.

5 Watch Where You're Going!

Antonio and Sonia
In the school hallway

Antonio: Hey, what are you doing?

Sonia: Oops. I'm sorry.

Antonio: Look at my shirt! It has your pen marks all over my sleeve!

Sonia: I'm sorry. I guess I wasn't looking where I was going.

Antonio: Well… *(The word is drawn out in a questioning tone.)*

Sonia: Here, let me get some soap and water.

CD - 19

VARIATION

5a (variation)
Antonio, Sonia, and Darlene
In the school hallway

Antonio: Hey, what are you doing?

Sonia: Oops. I'm sorry.

Antonio: Look at my books! They're all over the floor.

Sonia: I'm sorry. I guess I wasn't looking where I was going.

Antonio: Well… *(The word is drawn out in a questioning tone.)*

Sonia: Here, let me help you pick them up.

Antonio: Never mind. I've got them. *(Antonio leaves and Darlene comes up.)*

Darlene: What was the matter with him?

Sonia: Oh, I bumped into him and knocked his books on the floor.

Darlene: He seemed pretty mad.

Sonia: It was only a few books. And I didn't break anything.

Darlene: I heard you say you were sorry.

Sonia: Well, maybe he is having a bad day.

EXPANSION

Make a list of polite things you could say after you bump into someone or damage something. Check with your teacher to see if there are any others you might want to know.

6 Waiting in Line

Sam and Enrico

In school

Sam: Where are you going?

Enrico: To get my school ID.

Sam: So am I. I'll walk with you.

Enrico: Which line should we wait in, the left or the right one?

Sam: Hmmm... Let's try the right one.

Enrico: OK.

Sam: What should we do when we finish here?

Enrico: We should go back to social studies, of course.

Sam: I guess so. But it's almost lunchtime. And...

Enrico: And what?

Sam: I don't think our line is moving.

Enrico: Uh-oh. You're right. I think we chose the wrong line.

Sam: Should we try the other line?

Enrico: I don't think that one's moving, either. Looks like we'll miss social studies.

Sam: I sure hope we don't miss lunch!

6a (continuation)
In the school cafeteria

Enrico: Another line!

Sam: Yeah, but for a better reason. What are you having?

Enrico: I think I'll have a hamburger, french fries, and milk. What about you?

Sam: I'm going to have a cheeseburger, a small salad, and chocolate milk.

Enrico: Finally! The line is moving!

EXPANSION

Think of all the times you have had to wait in line. Which time was the longest? Share your story with friends.

7 Bad News

CD - 21

Billy, Susan, and Jimmy
In the playground

Susan:	Billy, why are you crying?
Billy:	I'm not crying. *(Billy's voice quavers a bit.)*
Susan:	Yes, you are. What's the matter?
Billy:	My hamster died.
Susan:	Oh, Billy. I'm so sorry!
Billy:	It's OK.
Susan:	I know how you feel.
Billy:	You do?
Susan:	I had a puppy once. He got hit by a car.
Billy:	Did he die?
Susan:	Yeah. I cried for a week!
Billy:	You did?
Susan:	Yeah. I still miss him sometimes.
Billy:	*(Billy wipes his tears.)* Thanks, Susan. *(Billy leaves. Jimmy comes up.)*
Jimmy:	I heard what you said, Susan. That was nice.
Susan:	Do you think so?
Jimmy:	You made him feel better.

7a (variation)

Susan:	Billy, why are you crying?
Billy:	I'm not crying. *(Billy's voice quivers a bit.)*
Susan:	Yes, you are. What's the matter?
Billy:	My mother lost her job.
Susan:	Oh, Billy. I'm so sorry!
Billy:	It's OK.
Susan:	I know how you feel.
Billy:	You do?
Susan:	My sister lost her job last month.
Billy:	Did she get another job?
Susan:	Yeah, but we all worried a lot.
Billy:	You did?
Susan:	You bet we did. She really needs to work.

EXPANSION

Tell your classmates or teacher of bad news that came to you at some time. Did anyone make you feel better? Tell about a time you tried to help someone feel better about bad news.

8 Let's Go See the Teacher

Christopher and Zach
Walking home from school

Christopher:	This is going to be hard.
Zach:	What?
Christopher:	Our homework for Monday.
Zach:	Oh, not so hard.
Christopher:	Easy for you to say.
Zach:	You just have to read a book and write a paragraph.
Christopher:	Sure, read a book! A whole book! Do you know how long that will take me?
Zach:	Hmm… Let's think about this.
Christopher:	OK.
Zach:	Did the teacher say what kind of book?
Christopher:	No, just a book.
Zach:	Well. Look, I know you're not a baby, but what about reading a baby book?
Christopher:	A baby book?
Zach:	Sure. Why not?
Christopher:	Well, like what?
Zach:	Let's go to the library after school. I'll show you what I mean.
Christopher:	OK. Thanks. I'll try anything.

8a (variation)

Christopher:	This is going to be hard.
Zach:	What?
Christopher:	Our homework for Monday.
Zach:	Oh, not so hard.
Christopher:	Easy for you to say.
Zach:	You just have to read a book and write a paragraph.
Christopher:	Sure, read a book! A whole book! Do you know how long that will take me?
Zach:	Hmm… Let's think about this.
Christopher:	OK.
Zach:	Did you explain to the teacher that a whole book is too hard for you?
Christopher:	No, I really didn't want to.

Zach:	Well. Look, you really have to talk to the teacher.
Christopher:	Will you come with me?
Zach:	Sure. Why not?
Christopher:	Great!
Zach:	Let's go see the teacher before school tomorrow.
Christopher:	OK. Thanks. I'll try anything.

8b (continuation)

Christopher, Zach, and Mr. Shaw

In school the next morning

Mr. Shaw:	Good morning, Zach. Oh, and good morning to you, too, Christopher.
Zach:	Good morning, Mr. Shaw.
Mr. Shaw:	You two are here early.
Zach:	Yes. Christopher has a problem.
Mr. Shaw:	A problem?
Christopher:	About the homework.
Mr. Shaw:	What about the homework?
Christopher:	Well, it's too hard.
Mr. Shaw:	Too hard? How?
Christopher:	Zach, you explain.
Zach:	Sure. Mr. Shaw, Christopher needs an easier book. Or a shorter one.
Mr. Shaw:	Oh, of course. I forgot. Let's look over here.
Zach:	What are these?
Mr. Shaw:	These are good books, just not so long.
Christopher:	Look here! This one looks good.
Mr. Shaw:	Take it, and good luck!
Christopher:	Thanks, Mr. Shaw. And thanks, Zach.

EXPANSION

Have you had homework assignments that were too hard because you still need to learn more English? What did you do? Did teachers or other students help you? Share your experience with your teacher or classmates.

9 The Dog Ate My Homework

 CD - 23 *Thomas and Li*

On the sidewalk, in front of school

Thomas: Hey, Li, wait for me!

Li: Sure, but hurry up.

Thomas: That homework last night was terrible.

Li: Uh-oh… What homework?

Thomas: All those math problems.

Li: Math problems?

Thomas: Fifty of them.

Li: Oh, I'm in trouble now. I forgot.

Thomas: That's bad news.

Li: Yeah, and I forgot my homework last week, too.

Thomas: What are you going to tell the teacher?

Li: How about, "The dog ate my homework"?

Thomas: Sorry, friend, he'll never believe that one.

Li: How about, "I did it, but I left it home"?

Thomas: No. Sarah used that excuse yesterday.

Li: I guess I'll have to tell him the truth.

Thomas: Good idea. And then you'd better have a plan.

Li: A plan for what?

Thomas: To make up your homework. Because that's what the teacher will ask for.

EXPANSION

Have you ever forgotten your homework? Did you tell the truth? What would you say to your teacher? What excuse would you give? What promises would you make?

10 Swimming Lessons

Binh and Christopher
In the hallway and locker room

Binh:	Hi, Christopher. Do you have P.E. now?
Christopher:	Yes. I have swimming. But I don't know where the pool is.
Binh:	I'll show you. I have swimming too. Follow me.
Christopher:	Oh, thanks.
Binh:	Here's the locker room.
Christopher:	Uh-oh. I didn't bring a lock.
Binh:	That's OK. Put your stuff in my locker for today.
Christopher:	Thank you. I'll do that.
Binh:	Now we take a shower and head for the pool.

10a (continuation)
In the pool

Christopher:	Ohhh! It's so cold!
Binh:	Yeah, but it will get warmer as we move around.
Christopher:	Did you take swimming lessons last year?
Binh:	Yeah. I've been swimming for a long time.
Christopher:	Well, this is my first time.
Binh:	Your first time?
Christopher:	Yes. It scares me a little.
Bihn:	Well, you'll do fine. Listen carefully to what the teacher tells you.
Christopher:	I will.
Binh:	And I'll stay near you to help explain things.

EXPANSION

It's often hard to do new things, but if someone helps you, it's a lot easier. Has anyone helped you do something new? Describe how someone helped you to your teacher.

11 After School

CD - 25

Margaret and Coach Brown
In the hallway

Coach Brown: Margaret, you're a great basketball player.

Margaret: Yes, Coach Brown. I know. I played basketball in Puerto Rico. I love basketball.

Coach Brown: It shows. I want you to try out for the basketball team.

Margaret: Hmmm…

Coach Brown: What?

Margaret: Practice is after school, right?

Coach Brown: Right. Until 6 o'clock.

Margaret: I'm sorry, I can't.

Coach Brown: Why not?

Margaret: I have to baby-sit my little brother after school.

Coach Brown: Can't someone else?

Margaret: No, there's only me.

11a (variation)
Vasili and Coach Brown
In the hallway

Coach Brown: Vasili, you're a good soccer player.

Vasili: Yes, Coach Brown. I know. I played soccer in Greece. I love soccer.

Coach Brown: It shows. I want you to try out for the soccer team.

Vasili: Yes! Of course!

Coach Brown: Come after school today.

Vasili: I'll be there!

EXPANSION

After school activities are important to many students. Do you do something after school? Try to write a dialogue between you and a friend about your favorite after school activity.

12 It Isn't Fair!

Jennifer and Margaret
On the telephone

Jennifer: Hello?

Margaret: Hi, it's Margaret. I'm so mad.

Jennifer: Mad? Why?

Margaret: Coach Brown wants me on the basketball team.

Jennifer: That's great! Why are you mad?

Margaret: Because I can't play.

Jennifer: Why not?

Margaret: They practice every day after school.

Jennifer: So?

Margaret: Think about it.

Jennifer: Oh… I remember… Your little brother Joey.

Margaret: You got it.

Jennifer: Couldn't your big brother Diego help?

Margaret: Diego, help? Fat chance!

Jennifer: Well, why not?

Margaret: He plays football after school.

Jennifer: You know, it's just not fair.

Margaret: Why do girls have to take care of the kids…

Jennifer: while the boys play?

12a (variation)

Jennifer: Hello?

Margaret: Hi, it's Margaret. I'm so mad.

Jennifer: Mad? Why?

Margaret: Mrs. Green wants me to join the art club.

Jennifer: That's great! Why are you mad?

Margaret: Because I can't.

Jennifer: Why not?

Margaret: They meet on Mondays after school.

Jennifer: So?

Margaret: Think about it.

Jennifer: Oh… I remember… Your little brother Joey.

Margaret: You got it.

Jennifer: Couldn't your big brother Diego help?

Margaret:	Diego, help? Fat chance!
Jennifer:	Well, why not?
Margaret:	He plays football after school.
Jennifer:	You're right. It's just not fair.
Margaret:	Why do girls have to take care of the kids...
Jennifer:	while the boys play?

12b (continuation)

Margaret, Mrs. Hernandez, and Mr. Hernandez
At the dinner table

Mr. Hernandez:	Margaret, you're quiet tonight.
Margaret:	Uh-hum.
Mr. Hernandez:	Is something on your mind?
Margaret:	No, not really.
Mrs. Hernandez:	Yes, there is. We can tell.
Margaret:	It's not important.
Mrs. Hernandez:	I think it is.
Margaret:	Mom, Dad, you know I love little Joey.
Mrs. Hernandez:	Of course, we all do.
Margaret:	But sometimes I feel mad.
Mr. Hernandez:	Why, Margaret?
Margaret:	Because I have to come home after school every day.
Mr. Hernandez:	Well, yes, you do...
Mrs. Hernandez:	Is that a problem?
Margaret:	Not really.
Mrs. Hernandez:	Come on, Margaret, tell us what's bothering you.
Margaret:	I want to join the art club!
Mrs. Hernandez:	And?
Margaret:	It meets every Monday after school.
Mr. Hernandez:	Oh, I see.
Margaret:	And it's not fair that Diego can play football and I can't have one day for me!
Mr. Hernandez:	Ah...
Mrs. Hernandez:	I see...

EXPANSION

What do you think will happen next? What will Margaret's mom and dad say and do? What will Diego say and do?

0-7682-3076-4   *Let's Chat: ESL Dialogues*

13 The Newcomer

Francisco and Ali
Outside school

Francisco:	Hi. I'm Francisco. I'm in your class.
Ali:	Hi. *(very quietly)*
Francisco:	Are you waiting for the bus?
Ali:	Yes.
Francisco:	Do you know what number?
Ali:	Number?
Francisco:	Everybody takes a different number bus, like 1, 2, 3.
Ali:	I don't know. I don't understand.
Francisco:	Let's ask Mr. Johnson.

13a (continuation)

Francisco, Ali, and Mr. Johnson

Francisco:	Mr. Johnson, Ali doesn't know his bus.
Mr. Johnson:	Let me check my list. *(pause)* He's on Bus 14.
Francisco:	Oh, no! It's just leaving!
Mr. Johnson:	You're right. Don't worry. We'll call his mother and find him a way home.
Francisco:	Thanks, Mr. Johnson. Ali, do you understand?
Ali:	I want to go home.

13b (continuation)

Francisco and Ali
The next day, in the hallway

Francisco:	Hi. Did you get home OK?
Ali:	Yes. My mom came.
Francisco:	Will you wait for the bus today?
Ali:	Yes.
Francisco:	I'll wait with you, OK?
Ali:	OK.
Francisco:	Do you want to eat lunch at my table?
Ali:	OK. At 11:30.
Francisco:	That's right. We eat lunch at 11:30. See you then!
Ali:	*(hesitantly practicing English)* See you…

EXPANSION

When you were new to this school, what things did you have to learn? Explain some of your experiences to your teacher and your classmates. What people were most helpful to you?

14 It's the Wrong Bus!

Ellen and Tracy (neighbors)
Getting on the school bus

Ellen:	Let's sit here, Tracy.
Tracy:	OK, Ellen.
Ellen:	Wasn't P.E. class fun today?
Tracy:	Yeah, especially because our team won.
Ellen:	Maybe we can play a little baseball when we get home.
Tracy:	Not me. I have to do my homework first.
Ellen:	Too bad.
Tracy:	Well, I don't mind much.
Ellen:	Maybe we can find some guys and play after dinner.
Tracy:	That sounds good to me.
Ellen:	Hey, wait a minute.
Tracy:	What?
Ellen:	Look around the bus.
Tracy:	So?
Ellen:	Do you see anyone you know?
Tracy:	Well....
Ellen:	I don't.
Tracy:	Me, neither.
Ellen:	Is that Mr. Claude?
Tracy:	Our bus driver? Nope.
Ellen:	I think we got on the wrong bus.
Tracy:	What do we do now?
Ellen:	I don't know.
Tracy:	Where are we?
Ellen:	I don't know. I have no idea.
Tracy:	Now what do we do?

14a (continuation)

Ellen:	I'm so embarrassed.
Tracy:	How did this happen?
Ellen:	We were thinking about baseball...
Tracy:	and not about getting on the right bus.

Ellen: So what do we do now?

Tracy: I don't know.

Ellen: We're going to have to do something.

Tracy: When?

Ellen: Not now. Let's wait.

Tracy: OK, but there are only two other people left.

Ellen: I know.

Tracy: We're going to have to do something soon.

Ellen: I know.

Tracy: There go the last people. Maybe we should just get off here.

Ellen: But we don't know where we are!

Tracy: I guess we're going to have to ask for help.

14b (continuation)

Tracy, Ellen, and Mrs. Schmidt

Mrs. Schmidt: Girls, what are you doing here?

Ellen: I'm sorry. We're lost.

Mrs. Schmidt: Don't cry, little girl.

Tracy: *(between sobs)* I can't help it.

Mrs. Schmidt: Where do you live?

Ellen: We live on Blossom Avenue.

Mrs. Schmidt: Well, you are a long way from home.

Tracy: *(still in tears)* We are?

Ellen: How are we going to get home?

Mrs. Schmidt: You won't believe this, but I have lost children on my bus almost every week.

Ellen: You do?

Mrs. Schmidt: Yes, all the buses look the same. Do you know your telephone number?

Tracy: Of course, we're not babies.

Mrs. Schmidt: Sorry, I didn't mean that. Let's call your parents so they won't worry. Then we'll decide what to do next.

Ellen
and Tracy: Oh, thank you.

EXPANSION

Did you ever get on the wrong bus? Or did you suddenly discover that you were lost? How did you feel? Talk about it with your teacher or with another student.

THE WIDER WORLD

1 Come On, Let's Play

Amelia and Vincent

At the park

Amelia: Come on, Vincent. Let's play soccer!

Vincent: OK. I'll teach you how.

Amelia: I'll kick the ball to you.

Vincent: OK.

Amelia: Ready? Here it comes!

            (sound of soccer ball being kicked)

Vincent: Ouch! You almost knocked me over!

Amelia: Sorry.

Vincent: You need to aim carefully, not just kick it hard.

Amelia: I did aim. It went right at you, didn't it?

Vincent: Yes, but... Maybe you were just lucky.

Amelia: OK. I'll kick it more gently next time.

Vincent: Good. You're learning.

Amelia: Here it comes. Ready?

Vincent: I think so.

1a (variation)
In the gym

Amelia: Come on, Vincent. Let's play basketball!

Vincent: OK. I'll teach you how.

Amelia: I'll pass the ball to you.

Vincent: OK, then I'll shoot.

Amelia: Ready? Here it comes.

Vincent: Ouch! You almost knocked me over!

Amelia: Sorry.

Vincent: You need to aim carefully. Not just throw hard.

Amelia: I did aim. It went right at you, didn't it?

Vincent: Yes, but... Maybe you were just lucky.

Amelia: OK. I'll aim more carefully next time.

0-7682-3076-4   *Let's Chat: ESL Dialogues*

Vincent: Good.
Amelia: Now. Teach me how to shoot.
Vincent: OK. Stand like this. Hold the ball up, bend your knees a little, and push the ball up toward the basket.
Amelia: You missed. Let me try it.
Vincent: OK. Do it like I told you.
Amelia: OK. Let's see. Hold the ball up… Bend your knees a little… Am I doing it right?
Vincent: Yes.
Amelia: And push the ball up toward the basket. Like that!
Vincent: Great shot! It went in on your first try!
Amelia: You're a great teacher, Vincent!

1b (variation)
At the bowling alley

Amelia: Come on, Vincent. Let's go bowling. Teach me how.
Vincent: Uh, to tell the truth, Amelia, I've never bowled before.
Amelia: Oh! I have. I'll teach you then.
Vincent: Do you think you can?
Amelia: Sure. First you take three steps, like this.
Vincent: Yeah…
Amelia: Then you let your arm swing back, and then forward.
Vincent: OK.
Amelia: Then roll the ball down the alley. Here, I'll show you.
Vincent: Oh, that was good, Amelia! It went right into that gutter along the side.
Amelia: Umm… It's not supposed to do that, Vincent. That was a gutter ball. It's supposed to stay right in the middle of the alley and knock over the pins, down at the end.
Vincent: Oh. You missed, then.
Amelia: Yes. Here, now you try.
Vincent: OK. Let your arm swing back, and then forward. Right?
Amelia: Yes. Good. Good.
Vincent: Then roll the ball down the alley. There it goes!
Amelia: Vincent! It's going right down the middle!
Vincent: That's good, isn't it?
Amelia: It's great! It's… It's going… You knocked down all ten pins! It's a strike! That's a wonderful shot!
Vincent: You're a great teacher, Amelia!

EXPANSION

What is your favorite sport? Explain how to do something in it, like kicking a soccer ball or shooting a basket. Get your teacher or a friend to try doing exactly what you say.

0-7682-3076-4   *Let's Chat: ESL Dialogues*

2 Forty Different Flavors!

Fred and Jesse
Outside school

Fred: Hey, let's walk home today.

Jesse: Not take the bus?

Fred: No, it's a nice day. And besides…

Jesse: Besides what?

Fred: I'm hungry!

Jesse: Me, too. But walking makes me hungrier.

Fred: Guess who has four dollars?

Jesse: You do?

Fred: I certainly do.

Jesse: Sounds like ice cream to me.

Fred: You are so right.

Jesse: Yum.

2a (continuation)
At the ice cream store

Fred: Gee, look at all the choices!

Jesse: One, two, three, four, five…

Fred: Six, seven, eight, nine, ten…

Jesse: Eleven, twelve, thirteen, fourteen, fifteen…

Fred: There must be forty flavors!

Jesse: Yum, yum, yum.

Fred: I probably like them all.

Jesse: Not me. I don't like ice cream with nuts.

Fred: Then don't get pistachio.

Jesse: Or maple walnut.

Fred: I think I'll try something new.

Jesse: Like what?

Fred: Look at that one. Bubble gum.

Jesse: Is there real bubble gum in it?

Fred: I think so. I'm going to try it.

Jesse: Me, too.

EXPANSION

Write the names of ten ice cream flavors. Tell someone your favorite. Ask others what their favorites are.

3 Doing Errands

Bill and Jack
On the sidewalk

Bill: Jack, want to go to the store with me?

Jack: Why?

Bill: My mom needs some groceries.

Jack: I guess so. Will it take long?

Bill: I don't think so. As soon as I'm finished, we can go play basketball.

CONTINUATION
CD - 31

3a (continuation)
In the store

Bill: Let's get a small cart.

Jack: Do you remember what you have to get?

Bill: There are only five things: milk, rice, lettuce, sugar, and...and...and... I can't remember!

Jack: Was it flour?

Bill: No!

Jack: Was it cheese?

Bill: No!

Jack: Was it oil?

Bill: Yes! Thanks for helping me remember!

Bill: It looks like we have everything.

Jack: Did you bring extra money?

Bill: A little.

Jack: Let's get some candy.

Bill: I'd prefer gum.

Jack: Do you have enough money for both?

Bill: Yes. Will you help me carry a bag, please?

Jack: Sure!

EXPANSION

Make a list of ten things you could buy at a grocery store. Share your list with your teacher and talk about what other things you might buy.

4 Laundry Day

Chuck (older brother) and Joshua (younger brother)

At the laundromat

Joshua: Whoa, Chuck, this laundry is heavy!

Chuck: Here Josh, I'll help.

Joshua: Thanks. There's a table.

Chuck: Good. I'll put it there.

Chuck: OK. You sort.

Joshua: Can do.

Chuck: I'll get the money ready.

Joshua: Hmmm... Is this shirt light or dark?

Chuck: Let's call it dark.

Joshua: How about these pants?

Chuck: Oh, definitely light.

Joshua: You're right. What was I thinking?

Chuck: How many machines will we need?

Joshua: Three, I think. Look at all the dark stuff.

Chuck: You're right. Yep. Two dark. One light.

4a (continuation)

Chuck: Let's see, then. One machine, four quarters.

Joshua: So three machines... twelve quarters.

Chuck: Hmmm (Sound of coins clinking)...yes...we have twelve quarters.

Joshua: Good. Now what about soap?

Chuck: Oops. Soap. I forgot.

Joshua: Looks like fifty cents for soap.

Chuck: Two quarters.

Joshua: And three machines.

Chuck: That's six more quarters.

Joshua: Twelve plus six. Do we have eighteen quarters?

Chuck: Let me count: two, four, six, eight, ten, twelve, fourteen. Nope.

Joshua: We need change.

Chuck: You ask.

Joshua: No, you!

Chuck: No, you!

Joshua: Come on, you're older!

Chuck: OK, but next time, you ask.

EXPANSION

Does your family do their laundry at home or at a laundromat? Who does the laundry? Do they sort by light and dark, as Chuck and Joshua do? If you go to a laundromat, how much does it cost?

5 Decisions, Decisions

Ramon and Tim

On the telephone

Ramon:	Hello?
Tim:	Hi, Ramon, it's Tim.
Ramon:	Hi. What are you doing?
Tim:	Not much.
Ramon:	Me neither.
Tim:	But I worked hard this morning.
Ramon:	You did?
Tim:	Yep.
Ramon:	Doing what?
Tim:	I helped my neighbor clean his basement.
Ramon:	Well, that doesn't sound too interesting.
Tim:	Not very, but my neighbor is nice. And he gave me five dollars for helping.
Ramon:	Five dollars! What are you going to do with it?
Tim:	Well, my father always says to save some and spend some.
Ramon:	Good idea. Do you need any help spending?
Tim:	*(laughing)* Sure. Let's go to the corner store.

5a (continuation)

Ramon, Tim, and Mrs. Mehta

At the corner store

Ramon and Tim:	*(in unison)* Hello, Mrs. Mehta.
Mrs. Mehta:	Hello, children. May I help you?
Tim:	Do you have any of those little cars?
Mrs. Mehta:	The little racing cars?
Tim:	Yes, those.
Mrs. Mehta:	Hmm… Let me see. Here's one.
Tim:	Oh, I already have that one.
Ramon:	But I don't. Can I hold it, please?
Mrs. Mehta:	Certainly, Ramon. Here it is.
Ramon:	Oh, that's neat. How much is it?
Mrs. Mehta:	Just two dollars.

Tim:	Let me think. Mrs. Mehta, you don't have any other racing cars?
Mrs. Mehta:	Hmm... Let me look under the counter. *(pause)* Oh, look, I found a whole new box!
Tim:	Wow! Look at these!
Ramon:	Look at the yellow racing car!
Tim:	And the green one!
Ramon:	And the black one!
Tim:	Wow! Let's get all three!
Ramon:	We can't.
Tim:	Why not?
Ramon:	Two dollars each. Three cars.
Tim:	Oh, you're right. We'd need six dollars.
Ramon:	Now what do we do?
Tim:	We have to make a decision.
Ramon:	Which one do you like better, green or black?
Tim:	I think the black one. Which one do you like?
Ramon:	Hmm... I think the yellow one.
Tim:	OK, let's get the black and yellow cars.
Ramon:	And then we have a dollar left for candy!

5b (continuation)

Ramon and Tim

Walking home

Tim:	Two cars to play with.
Ramon:	And candy to eat. Life is good.
Tim:	Uh-oh.
Ramon:	What?
Tim:	I forgot.
Ramon:	Forgot what?
Tim:	I spent the whole five dollars! I'm supposed to save some!

EXPANSION

What would you buy if you had five dollars? Tell a friend, and ask what your friend would buy.

6 Get a Job!

Vicki (younger sister) and Benjamin (older brother)

At home

Vicki:	You're so lucky.
Benjamin:	Lucky? Why?
Vicki:	You have a job.
Benjamin:	Well, you can have one, too. When you're older.
Vicki:	But I want a job now.
Benjamin:	Why?
Vicki:	Dad won't buy me any CDs.
Benjamin:	Well, CDs aren't really necessary.
Vicki:	True, but I want some.
Benjamin:	I see the problem. Let's think about jobs.
Vicki:	How? I'm too young.
Benjamin:	Well, too young for lots of jobs. But maybe there's something…

6a (variation)

Vicki:	You're so lucky.
Benjamin:	Lucky? Why?
Vicki:	You have a job.
Benjamin:	Well, you can have one, too. When you're older.
Vicki:	But I want a job now.
Benjamin:	Why?
Vicki:	Dad won't buy me another pair of sneakers.
Benjamin:	Well, you already have some.
Vicki:	True, but I want new ones.
Benjamin:	I see the problem. Let's think about jobs.
Vicki:	How? I'm too young.
Benjamin:	Well, too young for lots of jobs. But maybe there's something…

6b (continuation)

Benjamin:	Look out the window.
Vicki:	Yeah…
Benjamin:	What do you see?
Vicki:	What do you mean?

Benjamin: Well... Just look.

Vicki: Trees...

Benjamin: And?

Vicki: Grass...

Benjamin: And?

Vicki: Leaves.

Benjamin: Leaves. Where?

Vicki: Well, mostly on the ground.

Benjamin: Does that give you any ideas?

Vicki: Leaves. Raking?

Benjamin: I'll bet you could rake leaves for the neighbors.

Vicki: For money?

Benjamin: Why not?

6c (variation)

Benjamin: Look out the window.

Vicki: Yeah...

Benjamin: What do you see?

Vicki: What do you mean?

Benjamin: Well... Just look.

Vicki: Snow.

Benjamin: And?

Vicki: More snow.

Benjamin: And?

Vicki: Lots of snow.

Benjamin: Does that give you any ideas?

Vicki: Snow! Shoveling!

Benjamin: I'll bet you could shovel snow for the neighbors.

Vicki: For money?

Benjamin: Why not?

EXPANSION

You have to be 18 years old for many jobs, but not for all. What jobs could you do?

7 A Family Picnic

Peter, Margarita, little Alfonso, Mr. Garcia, and Mrs. Garcia
At home

Mrs. Garcia:	What a beautiful day!
Mr. Garcia:	Yes, it is. A great day for a picnic.
Children:	*(together)* Yaayy! A picnic in the park!
Peter:	Let's have hamburgers.
Margarita:	No, hot dogs!
Alfonso:	I want a peanut butter sandwich.
Margarita:	A peanut butter sandwich?
Peter:	That's weird.
Alfonso:	I like peanut butter sandwiches.
Mrs. Garcia:	Now, children, Alfonso can have what he wants.
Mr. Garcia:	But for the rest of us, what?
Mrs. Garcia:	Hamburgers or hot dogs.
Peter:	Hamburgers!
Margarita:	Hot dogs!
Mr. Garcia:	How about both?
Children:	Yaayy!

7a (continuation)

The family plus Mr. Mimberg, grocer
Mr. Mimberg's store

EXPANSION

Does your family go on picnics? Where do they go? What do they eat? Do they cook, or bring cold food?

Do you think Alfonso will share his sandwiches? Write or say the next part of the story.

Alfonso:	Hi Mr. Mimberg!
Mr. Mimberg:	Hello Alfonso. I see you have your whole family with you.
Mr. Garcia:	We came to pick up some hot dogs and hamburgers.
Peter:	We're going on a picnic!
Mr. Mimberg:	Well, it's a fine day for a picnic.
Margarita:	We'll need ketchup and mustard, too. And rolls. Enough for everybody.
Peter:	Except Alfonso!
Mr. Mimberg:	Alfonso is not eating today?
Peter:	He's having peanut butter sandwiches.
Margarita:	On a picnic! Have you ever heard anything so weird?
Alfonso:	I like peanut butter sandwiches!
Mr. Mimberg:	So do I, Alfonso! Have a great picnic, everybody!

7b (continuation)
In the park

Mrs. Garcia: OK, here we are.

Mr. Garcia: Let's find a grill.

Mrs. Garcia: There's one... Over there.

Children: Can we play?

Mr. Garcia: Sure, you can play. We'll cook.

Mrs. Garcia: Let's see... Hamburger meat, hot dogs, and two peanut butter sandwiches.

Mr. Garcia: Uh-oh.

Mrs. Garcia: What?

Mr. Garcia: I forgot charcoal. What an idiot I am!

Mrs. Garcia: No, dear, that's ok.

Mr. Garcia: Well, at least the kids can play.

Mrs. Garcia: Two peanut butter sandwiches. Five of us.
Do you think Alfonso will share?

Published by Frank Schaffer Publications. Copyright Protected.   0-7682-3076-4   *Let's Chat: ESL Dialogues*

8 Lost Something?

Emilio and Julio

On the sidewalk

Emilio: Hi, Julio. You look funny. Are you OK?

Julio: Not really, Emilio. I lost something.

Emilio: You? But you never do anything irresponsible!

Julio: I did this time. I lost my wallet.

Emilio: Wow! Do you remember the last time you had it?

Julio: Yeah, I was buying a CD at the mall and when I got home, I couldn't find it.

Emilio: That's too bad. Did you have a lot of money in it?

Julio: No, only about three dollars. But there was something more important in it.

Emilio: What?

Julio: A photo of my grandparents. It can never be replaced. My mom is going to be really upset with me.

8a (variation)

Clara and Maya

Walking home, after school

Clara: What's wrong, Maya?

Maya: I'm really mad. Someone broke into my locker at school.

Clara: Did they do anything to your stuff?

Maya: Yeah, they took all my books and tore the pages. Then, they left a mess on the floor near my locker. The worst part is that my CD player is gone.

Clara: What will you do next?

Maya: I'm not sure. I think I should tell the principal. Will you come with me tomorrow?

Clara: Sure. I'll be glad to help.

EXPANSION

Have you ever lost anything important? Talk with your friends about losing things and then finding them (or not finding them).

9 Say Cheese!

Lana and Danielle
On the sidewalk

Lana: Smile!

Danielle: What are you doing?

Lana: Taking your picture.

Danielle: Do we need a flash?

Lana: I don't think so because we're outside. Say "cheese."

Danielle: Say what?

Lana: Say "cheese." It helps you to smile.

9a (variation)

Lana: Smile!

Danielle: What are you doing?

Lana: Taking your picture.

Danielle: Should I stand here?

Lana: That looks great! Say "cheese!"

Danielle: Cheeeeeeeeeese!

Lana: Very good! Very nice smile.

9b (continuation)
The following week

Danielle: What are you looking at?

Lana: The pictures I took last week.

Danielle: Hey, I look pretty good!

Lana: And you're smiling!

Danielle: It works!

Lana: What?

Danielle: Saying "cheese." I said it and I smiled.

EXPANSION

Why does saying "cheese" help you smile?

10 Pay Attention to the Food!

John and Tony
In the kitchen at John's house

John: Want to watch the soccer game tonight?

Tony: Sure! Who's playing?

John: The U.S. women's team against Iceland.

Tony: Sounds great! Those women are terrific!

John: How about some ice cream? I've got some right here.

Tony: Sure! What flavor?

John: Mint chocolate chip. Here's a bowl for you… and here's a bowl for me.

Tony: Thanks!

John: Bring it into the living room. The game's about to start. *(pause)*

Tony: Half-time! And the score's tied at two all.

John: Would you like some more ice cream?

Tony: Sure!

John: Oh, no!

Tony: What's wrong?

John: I forgot to put the ice cream away! It will all be melted by now!

10a (variation)

Ruben and Patrick
In the kitchen at Ruben's house

Ruben: Want to watch a DVD?

Patrick: Sure! Which one?

Ruben: It's an old one, the one about buried pirate treasure.

Patrick: I've never seen that one.

Ruben: I've got some hot soup on the stove. Would you like some while we watch the movie?

Patrick: That would be great. I didn't have lunch.

Ruben: Here you are. A bowl of soup for you...and a bowl of
          soup for me.
          (a short time later)
Patrick: I smell something.
Ruben: What?
Patrick: Something burning.
Ruben: Something burning? *(sniffs the air)* Something burning!
          Oh, no! The soup is still on the stove! And I never
          turned it off!

EXPANSION

Describe a time when someone ruined a meal. Who was it and what did the person say about it?

11 Stranger Danger

CD - 39 *Alicia and Mrs. Thomas*

In the school hallway before class

Mrs. Thomas: Alicia! What's the matter, dear? You look so pale! And you're crying! Tell me what happened.

Alicia: I... I... Oh, Mrs. Thomas...

Mrs. Thomas: You're shaking! Hold my hand, dear. It's OK. You're here with me.

Alicia: A... A man... on the way to school...

Mrs. Thomas: Yes, dear. What happened?

Alicia: He followed me... in his car...

Mrs. Thomas: He followed you?

Alicia: He kept... He kept talking to me... *(She cries.)*

Mrs. Thomas: Come into the nurse's office. It's right here. It's OK. You're safe. As soon as you feel better, you can tell us what happened.

11a (continuation)

Alicia, Mrs. Thomas, and Mrs. McKim (the school nurse)

In the nurse's office

Mrs. Thomas: Mrs. McKim, Alicia's upset. She's had a scare.

Mrs. McKim: Come in here, Alicia, and sit down. Here, blow your nose. *(the sound of a nose blowing)* Now, can you tell me about it?

Alicia: A man...

Mrs. McKim: Yes?

Alicia: I think he was a bad man.

Mrs. McKim: What did he do?

Alicia: He was in a car. I was walking to school. He drove slowly, alongside of me.

Mrs. Thomas: Did he say anything to you?

Alicia: He asked me questions.

Mrs. McKim: Like what questions?

Alicia: Like... where's a gas station?

Mrs. McKim: And?

Alicia: And then he wanted me to get in the car.

Mrs. Thomas: Oh, dear! You didn't, did you? Smart girl!

Alicia:	I kept walking, but he kept driving alongside.
Mrs. McKim:	What else did he say?
Alicia:	He said he'd give me a ride to school. I started running… Then I got to school.

11b (continuation)

Mrs. McKim:	Mrs. Thomas, call Mr. Snyder and ask him to call the police.
Mrs. Thomas:	Right.
Mrs. McKim:	Alicia, it's going to be all right. Do you remember what the man looked like?
Alicia:	No…yes…well, sort of.
Mrs. Thomas:	What about the car?
Alicia:	It was yellow. With rust spots all over. An old car.
Mrs. McKim:	Alicia, you did everything right.
Mrs. Thomas:	The police will be here soon. And Mr. Snyder is on his way now.
Mrs. McKim:	They'll want to talk to you. Try to remember everything you can. We'll stay right here with you.
Alicia:	OK.
Mrs. Thomas:	Feel any better?
Alicia:	I'm still a little scared.
Mrs. McKim:	I would be too! But you're safe now, and you're going to be fine. And the police will get him. He won't bother you or anyone else again.

EXPANSION

Have you ever had a dangerous experience? What did you do? What should Alicia do the next time? What will Mrs. Thomas and Mrs. McKim do next?

12 Call 911!

Nicolas, Mrs. Wagner, and 911 dispatcher

Mrs. Wagner rushes into the house.

Mrs. Wagner: Nicolas! Quick—call 911!

Nicolas: What? Why?

Mrs. Wagner: Mr. Fenster next door fell down. Call 911.

Nicolas: 911?

Mrs. Wagner: Just those three numbers on the phone. 9, 1, 1.

Nicolas: OK.

Mrs. Wagner: Then tell them our address and tell them to send an ambulance right away.

Nicholas: *(going to the phone)* OK!

Mrs. Wagner: I'm going back out to help him. (She leaves.)

(Nicolas dials 911. Dialing tones.)

Dispatcher: 911. Where are you calling from?

Nicolas: My... my mom said to call—

Dispatcher: OK, son. What's your name?

Nicolas: Nicolas.

Dispatcher: How old are you, Nicolas?

Nicolas: Nine.

Dispatcher: What's your last name?

Nicolas: Wagner.

Dispatcher: Good. I'm going to ask you some more questions. Are you at home now?

Nicolas: Yes.

Dispatcher: Nicolas, what is your address?

Nicolas: Rockford Street.

Dispatcher: Good. Rockford Street. Do you know what number?

Nicolas: 32.

12a (continuation)

Nicholas and 911 dispatcher

Dispatcher: Good boy. Now, what happened?

Nicolas: Mr. Fenster fell down. He's really old. My mom said to call.

Dispatcher: Does Mr. Fenster live with you?

Nicolas: No, he lives next door. My mom went back to help.

Dispatcher: Is he awake and breathing?

Nicolas: I don't know. My mom said to get an ambulance.

Dispatcher: Is he in his house or outside?

Nicolas: I don't know.

Dispatcher: OK, Nicolas. An ambulance is on its way. But don't hang up the phone. I need to ask you more questions.

Nicolas: OK.

12b (continuation)

Dispatcher: Nicolas, did you say your mother is helping Mr. Fenster?

Nicolas: Yes, she went back out.

Dispatcher: Is she a doctor or a nurse?

Nicolas: No.

Dispatcher: OK. Now, what's your phone number?

Nicolas: OK. 555-8625.

Dispatcher: Do you know the area code?

Nicolas: Yes. It's 585.

Dispatcher: Good. Now I want you to go outside. Don't go in the street. Just stand on the sidewalk and watch for the ambulance.

Nicolas: OK. Will it come soon?

Dispatcher: Sure, and when you see it, wave so they know where to go.

EXPANSION

Dialing (or pressing) 911 works to get help anywhere in the United States. Write this on a piece of paper and put it near your telephone: 911, your telephone number, and your address. And practice saying a sentence or two, like "Hello, this is an emergency. I need help." Then you will be ready if you have an emergency.

13 The Birthday Party

Shari and Ana

At Shari's house

Shari: Hi, Ana. I'm glad you could come over.

Ana: Hi, Shari. I brought my birthday gift for Katrina.

Shari: I have mine too. It was nice of Katrina to invite us to her party.

Ana: And I'm glad you offered to help me wrap my gift. I don't think I know how.

Shari: I have everything we need: wrapping paper, scissors, tape, and ribbon.

Ana: OK. What do you do first?

Shari: First, measure the paper.

Ana: Then what?

Shari: Then cut it like this so it's a little bigger than the box.

Ana: Ah. I see.

Shari: Then I tape it at both ends.

Ana: It looks good! Is it finished now?

Shari: Almost. I'll put this ribbon on… Like this. There! Now we're done!

Ana: But don't we need a card?

Shari: I almost forgot! Let's make one ourselves and tape it to the outside.

Ana: Good idea.

Shari: There. You've seen me wrap mine. Now you go ahead and wrap yours.

EXPANSION

Describe a birthday party you have been to. What did everyone do? Were there presents? Were there games? Was there cake?

13a (continuation)

Shari, Ana, and Katrina

Katrina's house, at the party

Shari
and Ana: *(together)* Happy Birthday, Katrina!

Katrina: Oh, thank you for coming.

Shari: Here are your birthday presents.

Katrina: Oh, they're so beautifully wrapped!

Ana: Aren't you going to open them?

Katrina: Not yet. I will in a little while. But first we all have a piece of cake. My mom made it and it's yummy!

14 The Right Fit

Armando and David (brothers)
At the mall, in a dressing room

Armando:	How does it look?
David:	It's too big. The sleeves are too long.
Armando:	Do you want me to get you another one?
David:	Yeah. In blue.
Armando:	In blue? But I thought you liked red.
David:	I do, but I like blue just as well.
Armando:	OK, I'll look for one.
David:	Thanks. I'll be right here in the dressing room.
	(brief pause)
Armando:	Here you go. I found you a smaller size in blue.
David:	Thanks. I'll try it on. *(pause)* What do you think?
Armando:	That looks great!

CONTINUATION

CD - 42

14a (continuation)

Armando, David, and a saleswoman
In the mall, walking in front of a shoe store

Armando:	David, don't you need shoes?
David:	Yes, for the wedding.
Armando:	What kind do you need?
David:	Dress shoes to go with my suit.
Armando:	Here's a shoe store.
David:	Good. Let's look in the window first.
Armando:	What about those?
David:	Well, OK, but not brown.
Armando:	What color do you want?
David:	Black.
Armando:	OK. Let's go inside.
David:	*(to a saleswoman)* Excuse me, do you have these in a size 12?
Saleswoman:	Yes, we do. Sit over here and try them on.
David:	This feels pretty good. I'll take them.

Saleswoman:	Better try the other one on, too.
David:	Why?
Saleswoman:	Most people's feet are different sizes.
David:	Oh, I didn't know that
Saleswoman:	So, how does the other foot feel?
David:	Good enough. Do you take charge cards?

EXPANSION

What is most important to you in clothing? Color? Fit? Comfort? Style? What about shoes or sneakers? Which do you like best? Share your preferences with your friends and ask them what they like.

JUST FOR FUN

1 I'm Thinking of Something

Nadia and Elena
At Nadia's house

Elena:	I learned a new game, Nadia. Let's play.
Nadia:	How do you play it?
Elena:	First, I say, "I'm thinking of something." Then I give you a couple of clues. And you have to guess what it is.
Nadia:	OK, let's try it.
Elena:	I'm thinking of something yellow that is also a fruit.
Nadia:	That's easy! A banana.
Elena:	Right! Now you think of something.
Nadia:	OK. Let's see.
Elena:	Don't make it too hard.
Nadia:	I won't. OK. I'm thinking of an animal that has spots.
Elena:	I know! A leopard!
Nadia:	Yup. Your turn.

1a (continuation)

Elena:	I'm thinking of something…um…an animal that picks up food with its nose.
Nadia:	An anteater?
Elena:	Oh. Maybe you're right. But that's not the one I'm thinking of. I'm thinking of a *big* animal.
Nadia:	Oh, I know! An elephant!
Elena:	Right! Go ahead.
Nadia:	I'm thinking of something that has teeth, but it's not a person or an animal.
Elena:	*(thinking)* Something that has teeth, but it's not a person… or an animal. Oh boy. I don't know.

0-7682-3076-4 *Let's Chat: ESL Dialogues*

Nadia: You use it every day.

Elena: Oh! A fork?

Nadia: No silly. A fork doesn't have teeth.

Elena: Oh I know! A comb.

Nadia: You got it.

1b (continuation)

Elena: I've got one. I'm thinking of a flower that also has thorns.

Nadia: Um... What are *thorns*?

Elena: They're like. . .sharp needles on the stem. They stick you if you touch them.

Nadia: Ah. A rose.

Elena: Yup. OK. Just one more.

Nadia: OK. I'm thinking of something yellow that is also a fruit.

Elena: Hey. A banana! We did that already!

Nadia: No, we didn't.

Elena: Yes, we did.

Nadia: It's not a banana.

Elena: Not a banana? Hmmm... What else could it be?

Nadia: I'll give you a clue. You can use it to make a drink.

Elena: Hmmm...drink...yellow fruit...not a banana...

Nadia: A bigger clue, then. You use it to make lemonade.

Elena: Oh! Why didn't I think of that? A lemon!

EXPANSION

Try playing "I'm Thinking of Something" with your friends.

2 Categories

CD - 44

Nadia and Elena
At Elena's house

Elena: I'm glad you could come to my house today Nadia. We had fun with that game yesterday.

Nadia: Let's try a new game today. Remember the game called *Categories* that we played in school?

Elena: Yeah. You name three things, and I tell the category.

Nadia: Right. Here we go. Red, green, blue.

Elena: Easy. Colors.

Nadia: Right. Your turn.

Elena: Umm… Pine, oak, maple.

Nadia: Trees!

Elena: This is too easy.

Nadia: OK. I'll make it harder. Mice, gerbils, chipmunks, but *not* lions.

Elena: Animals! No, wait. *Small* animals. Oh, that was good.

2a (continuation)

Nadia: Now you try.

Elena: OK. Here's one. New York, Chicago, Los Angeles, but *not* London.

Nadia: Oh, that would be cities… but wait. London's a city. Oh, I know. Cities in the United States.

Elena: Right! OK, last one. Chocolate chip, milk.

Nadia: Huh? Wait. There's only two, and not three.

Elena: True enough.

Nadia: And chocolate chip is a cookie. But milk is milk—a drink. They're not a category. They don't go together!

Elena: Yes they do.

Nadia: How? What's the category?

Elena: The category is, what we're going to have, right now!

EXPANSION

Make cards with as many words and categories as you can think of. Then play the category game with your friends.

3 I Can Read Your Mind

Alan and George
At George's house

Alan: I can read your mind.

George: What do you mean?

Alan: You choose a number…

George: Yes….

Alan: And I can tell you what it is.

George: Oh, sure. How can you do that?

Alan: You'll see. Want to try?

George: Yep.

Alan: OK. First, let's get a calculator.

George: I have one somewhere. Just a minute.

Alan: I'll wait.

CD - 45 **3a (continuation)**

George: OK, here it is.

Alan: Good. Now, think of a number between one and ten.
But don't tell me.

George: OK. I got it.

Alan: Put it in your calculator.

George: It's in.

Alan: Multiply it by 5.

George: Done.

Alan: Add 6.

George: Yep.

Alan: Multiply by 4.

George: Uh-huh.

Alan: Add 9.

George: Are we done yet?

Alan: Not quite. Multiply by 5.

George: Got it.

Alan: OK. Read me the number you have in your calculator now.

George: Eight hundred sixty-five.

3b (continuation)

Alan: Let me think...

George: Well?

Alan: Don't rush me. I'm reading your mind...

George: I'm waiting.

Alan: OK! The number you chose is... Here, let me write it on a paper for you.

George: You're right! How did you know?

EXPANSION

You can read your friends' minds too! Here's how it works. When your friend gives you the number in his calculator, do this.

Take the number.

Subtract 165.

Forget the two 0s at the end.

The number you get is your friend's original number!

Here's an example.

Let's say your friend picks number 7.	*7*
Multiply it by 5.	*35*
Add 6.	*41*
Multiply by 4.	*164*
Add 9.	*173*
Multiply by 5.	*865*

Here is your secret.

Take the number your friend gave you.	*865*
Subtract 165.	*700*
Forget the 0s	*7*

You did it! It works with bigger numbers too! Now go show your friends that you can read their minds!

4 Riddles

 CD - 46 *Mario and Ivan*

At Mario's house

Mario: Ivan, do you know any good riddles?

Ivan: I don't think so. What's a riddle?

Mario: A riddle is a joke, where there's a question and a trick answer.

Ivan: Tell me one.

Mario: OK. What has four wheels and flies?

Ivan: Uh... I don't know.

Mario: A garbage truck!

Ivan: What? Garbage trucks can't fly!

Mario: That's the trick. It doesn't mean the trucks can fly. It means they *have* flies—you know, those little bugs that land on your arm. Flies like garbage.

Ivan: Oh, I get it now. All right. That was good.

4a (continuation)

Ivan: Tell me another riddle.

Mario: OK. What did the duck say when she bought the lipstick?

Ivan: Uh... I don't know again.

Mario: She said, *Put it on my bill.*

Ivan: Huh? You better explain that one too.

Mario: OK. Ducks have *bills*, you know, instead of a mouth and lips.

Ivan: OK, I get that part. But what's the joke?

Mario: *Bill* also means a piece of paper that tells how much money you owe when you buy something. *Put it on my bill* means write down how much I owe.

Ivan: Oh... Now I see. Hey, *bill* also means dollar bill!

Mario: You're right!

Ivan: So here's a riddle for you: What's good to have and *not* to have?

Mario: Um, let me think. How could it be both? Nope, I can't figure it out.

Ivan: A *bill!* A dollar bill that you want and a bill you don't want to pay.

Mario: Hey, that was great! You know what a riddle is now!

4b (continuation)
The next day in the school cafeteria

Ivan: Let's tell some more jokes while we're having lunch.

Mario: OK. Have you got one?

Ivan: Yup. Why did the chicken cross the road?

Mario: How should I know?

Ivan: To get to the other side.

Mario: That's a bad joke.

Ivan: I know, but try this one: Why did the chewing gum cross the road?

Mario: To get to the other side?

Ivan: Nope. It was stuck on the leg of the chicken.

Mario: Where did you hear these silly jokes?

Ivan: From my friends. They're weird.

Mario: OK, here's one: What kind of flowers do you have between your nose and your chin?

Ivan: I know: tulips. Two lips.

Mario: Right! What's the best month for a parade?

Ivan: I give up.

Mario: March!

Ivan: I should have gotten that! You *march* in a parade. Let's go out to the playground now.

Mario: Yes, but first, speaking of the playground: How can you cut the sea in two?

Ivan: I don't know.

Mario: With a seesaw!

EXPANSION

What riddles like these do you know? Try them on your friends. Get your friends to try some on you.

0-7682-3076-4   *Let's Chat: ESL Dialogues*

5 To the Seashore

Becky and Martin
In the school cafeteria

Becky: Martin, do you have a calculator?

Martin: Yes Becky, right here.

Becky: Here's a problem. Use your calculator.

Martin: OK.

Becky: You're going to go to the seashore.

Martin: I am?

Becky: Yes, and you wonder what you'll find there.

Martin: I do?

Becky: Yes. And you'll use your calculator to find out.

Martin: How can I do that?

Becky: You'll see.

5a (continuation)

Becky: To go to the seashore, you take the Number 4 bus.
         Put in a 4.

Martin: OK, I did.

Becky: And the seashore is 4 stops away. So add 4 to the 4
         you already have.

Martin: All right.

Becky: Now, at the first stop, a 9-year-old girl gets on the bus.
         So multiply what you have by 9.

Martin: Done. But this won't work.

Becky: Yes, it will. The girl has 1 freckle on her face. So add 1.

Martin: OK, but I think you're crazy.

5b (continuation)

Becky: At the second stop, a 7-year-old boy gets on. So
         multiply by 7.

Martin: OK, I did it. How is this going to tell me what I'll...

Becky: Don't worry, it will. Now, at the third stop, three more
         boys get on. They're all 10 years old, so multiply by 10
         for the first one...and by 10 again for the second...and
         by 10 again for the third.

Martin: Whatever you say, girl.

5c (continuation)

Becky: At the fourth stop, you get off. And you see a sign that says Beach 350 Feet.

Martin: So what do I do?

Becky: You add 350.

Martin: OK.

Becky: You figure it will take you about 5 minutes to walk to the beach. So subtract 5.

Martin: OK, now what?

Becky: That's all.

Martin: That's all?

Becky: That's all. What did you find at the beach?

Martin: I told you it wouldn't work! I got 5-1-1-3-4-5.

Becky: No, silly. Turn your calculator upside down.

Martin: Yeah…

Becky: Now read it to me.

Martin: I can't! It's upside d— Oh my gosh! Now I get it! How did you do that?

EXPANSION

Try this trick on your friends. Just follow the steps in the dialogue, but make sure your friend gets all the numbers right. You can make up a different story if you like. Just be sure to use the same numbers.

If you want to trick your friends even more, let them pick the first number, between 1 and 10. You just have to be sure that the next number you give them to put in the calculator gives you an 8. For example:

If your friends pick...	tell them to add...	
4	4	
7	1	
3	5	to get 8.

If your friends pick...	tell them to subtract...	
10	2	
15	7	to get 8.

Then keep all the other numbers the same. You'll have to change the story a little in the beginning. Just be creative!

0-7682-3076-4   *Let's Chat: ESL Dialogues*

Language Functions

The 1997 TESOL publication *ESL Standards for Pre-K–12 Students** sets forth goals and standards that are built around a functional approach to language learning. The dialogues in this book follow such an approach. While attempting to capture the kinds of subjects and situations young students actually talk about, the dialogues also reflect the range of functions that their language contains. Most language exchanges are multifunctional, that is, they express more than one function.

The table of functions below identifies most of the central and many of the peripheral functions of the language in this book's dialogues. Students and teachers wishing to focus on a particular function may use the table to quickly identify the corresponding dialogues.

The functions listed in the table are specific to this book. For the most part, however, they fall under the following goals and standards from *TESOL'S ESL Standards for Pre-K–12 Students.*

Goal 1:   To Use English to Communicate in Social Settings

    Standard 1:   Students will use English to participate in social interaction.

    Standard 2:   Students will interact in, through, and with spoken and written English for personal expression and enjoyment.

Goal 3:   To Use English in Socially and Culturally Appropriate Ways

    Standard 1:   Students will use the appropriate language variety, register and genre according to audience, purpose and setting.

*TESOL. (1997). ESL Standards for Pre-K–12 Students. Alexandria, VA: Author.

The numbers in the tables are dialogue numbers.

Exchanging information	Chapter 1 Home	Chapter 2 School	Chapter 3 The Wider World	Chapter 4 Just for Fun
Asking questions	2, 6, 9, 12	3		
Answering questions	2, 6, 9			
Giving/getting information	6	1, 2, 7, 8, 10, 13	5, 8, 10, 12, 14	
Giving details	2, 9	2	8, 11, 12	
Clarifying	8, 11	3		2, 4

Guiding and conducting action	Chapter 1 Home	Chapter 2 School	Chapter 3 The Wider World	Chapter 4 Just for Fun
Making plans		4, 6		
Making decisions		1, 6	11, 14	
Extending/accepting invitations			3, 10, 11	
Giving directions/instructions	8, 12		13	3, 5
Requesting	1	4	7	
Making demands	4			
Asking for help	2		8, 12	
Offering help	2, 4		8, 12	
Giving advice	5	9	1, 2, 9	
Exploring options			6, 14	
Solving problems		4, 8, 9, 13, 14	3, 4, 5, 6	
Disagreeing	3, 13			
Understanding culture	11, 12	11	6, 9, 11, 12	
Persuading	1, 4, 5, 11	1	2, 4, 10	
Reminding	7	4		

Expressing feelings and emotion	Chapter 1 Home	Chapter 2 School	Chapter 3 The Wider World	Chapter 4 Just for Fun
Expressing excitement	7, 10			
Expressing disappointment		4, 12	8	
Expressing displeasure	3	5, 11		
Empathizing	9, 10			
Reassuring, encouraging		8, 10, 11, 14		
Connecting	11	2, 7, 10, 13	1, 6, 8, 11, 12	1, 2, 3, 4, 5
Resisting	3, 4, 5, 11		11	
Expressing condolence		7		
Apologizing		5	1	
Joking, kidding, teasing	13			

Weaving creativity and insight	Chapter 1 Home	Chapter 2 School	Chapter 3 The Wider World	Chapter 4 Just for Fun
Telling jokes	4			
Playing games				1, 2